# The Lazy Gardener's
# GUIDE TO EASY FRUITS AND BERRIES

## Fruits and Berries Anyone Can Grow

**TREY WATSON**

 **The Lazy Gardener**

www.leggcreekfarm.com
www.lazygardener.co

copyright © Trey Watson
All rights reserved.

Printed in the United States of America.

ISBN: 978-0-9982272-3-8

No part of this book may be reproduced or transmitted in any form or by any means, graphic, electronic, or mechanical, including photocopying, recording, taping, or by any information storage retrieval system, without the permission, in writing, from the publisher.

**Legg Creek Publishing**
PO Box 43
Douglass, TX 75943

# CONTENTS

Introduction ............................................................... 1

Blackberry ................................................................. 5

Currants ................................................................... 15

Elderberry ................................................................ 25

Fig .......................................................................... 35

Goumi Berry ............................................................. 45

Honeyberry .............................................................. 53

Japanese (Oriental) Persimmon ................................ 63

Mahonia ................................................................... 75

Mulberry .................................................................. 85

Pomegranate ........................................................... 95

Surinam Cherry (Pitanga) ....................................... 105

Wild Blueberry ....................................................... 113

Acknowledgments .................................................. 121

Other Books by Trey Watson ................................... 122

About the Author .................................................... 123

To Chica, my beautiful wife, who lives life along side me and makes her mark on eternity like I never could.

# INTRODUCTION

Even in the age of automated houses, digital assistants, and 24/7 connectivity, there's something about the soil that calls to us. We have more access to information than any humans in history, but we feel busy, overworked, and stretched thin. For many people, the solution to that busyness is gardening. Even if they don't get to enjoy the garden and its produce as much as they would like, many people love the garden and the idea of growing flowers and food.

This book is the second in the *Lazy Gardener's Guide* series. After several years of trial and error and accidental success, I've identified a dozen fruit and berry plants that are much easier to grow than their counterparts. I had a few considerations when researching and experimenting with these plants. They were:

1. Ease of growth – Could almost anyone - with a little time and soil - grow this plant successfully?

2. Non-invasive – Is this plant going to be so easy to grow that it will displace native plants?

3. Is this plant suitable for growing in much of the world?

4. Can I grow it with little effort?

With a few tiny exceptions (that are mentioned in the book), the plants in this book are easy-to-grow, non-invasive, adapted to much of the world, and I (though not really an expert) could handle growing them with little effort. These are fun, easy-going plants that anyone can have success with.

These fruits and berries – and any garden plants – benefit from practices that require minimal work while providing extensive benefits. A few of these practices are:

**Mulching** – Mulching involves placing a layer of organic matter over the surface of bare soil. Dried leaves, dried grass clippings, aged hay, compost, aged bark, aged

shredded wood chips, and many other organic materials make excellent mulches. Mulching helps retain soil moisture, creating a favorable micro-climate for plant growth and beneficial soil microbes.

**Soil testing** – Most plants in this book grow in a wide variety of soil types, but soil testing can give you insight into your soil and what nutrients it needs for best plant growth and fruit production. In the United States, most land grant universities have soil testing programs. Small universities with agriculture programs may also have soil testing services.

**Drip irrigation** – Drip irrigation with timers can reduce your need for hand watering plants described in this book or any garden plants. Drip irrigation usually involves polyvinyl tubing laid out among plants, with small emitters extending out from the tube over the plants. This provides the benefit of water conservation and lower water bills. A timer on the water faucet, allowing the water to flow only on given days and for a limited time, will free up your time to work on other gardening projects.

Other practices are discussed in more detail in *The Lazy Gardener's Guide to Easy Edibles*.

It is my hope that you find these plants enjoyable and easy to grow. I hope that you get to taste the "fruit" of your effort as you enjoy what these plants produce.

As someone who grows plants for a living, I always enjoy learning about new plants or new gardening tips and techniques. I'd love to hear from you! If you have any comments or criticisms or lazy gardening tips you would like to share, would you email me at **sales@leggcreekfarm.com** ? You can also find me at my company's Facebook page (**http://www.facebook.com/LeggCreekFarm**) and on the company Instagram account (**@LeggCreekFarm**).

Good luck and happy Gardening!

*Trey Watson*

*May 2018*

# BLACKBERRY

Blackberries (*Rubus* sp.) are one of the most popular garden plants, and with good reason: they're easy to grow and tasty. Blackberries are widely cultivated and used in a variety of desserts, drinks, flavorings, and decorations. Species of *Rubus* are native to Asia, Europe, and the Americas. The first wild blackberries were probably first brought under cultivation in Asia or Eastern Europe; the ancient Greeks and Romans used them. Early settlers and Native Americans in North America selected the best-producing wild vines for cultivation. Modern blackberry breeding began in California in the 1880's. Today there are dozens of named varieties of blackberries and the typical thorniness associated with wild blackberries is absent in many modern varieties. Wild blackberries, commonly called dewberries in North America, are considered by many wildlife conservationists to be one of the most important food sources for animals. They are discussed in detail in *The Lazy Gardener's Guide to Easy Edibles*.

Medicinally, the blackberry is packed with benefits. Native Americans used every part of the plant for a variety of ailments, using both the berries and the leaves. Both are rich in vitamins C, B, K, E, and fiber. Antioxidants found in the plant, such as zeaxanthin and lutein, may fight the causes of chronic diseases and the effects of aging. The leaves are used as an anti-diuretic, and contain flavonoids that may aid in healing sores of the mouth, wounds, and sore throats.

There are three general types of blackberries: trailing, semi-erect, and erect. Trailing and semi-erect need trellises for support. Erect varieties support themselves. The most common varieties of blackberries are semi-erect and erect. Many great cultivars are readily available, and grow well in the temperate regions of the world.

A few common blackberry varieties are:

- **Arapaho** - Erect thornless; 400 to 500 chill hours; USDA zones 6-8; earliest ripening thornless variety.

- **Apache** - Erect thornless; 400 to 600 chill hours; USDA zones 5-9.

- **Natchez** - Semi-erect thornless; early ripening; USDA zones 4-9; 300 chill hours; hardy, great for colder areas; disease resistant.

- **Ouachita** - Erect thornless; USDA zones 5-9; 300-500 chill hours; disease resistant.

- **Prime Ark Freedom** - Thornless erect; Zones 5-9; very low chill hours, 100-150; world's first blackberry plant to produce fruit on both primocanes (first year's growth), and florocanes (second year's growth); early ripening, and if conditions are right, can produce twice in a season; disease resistant.

## Care and Cultivation

**Site Selection and Soil**

Blackberries grow best in fertile, well-draining soil with a slightly acidic pH (5.5-7 is optimal). For best results, till in organic matter two weeks prior to planting to enrich soil. Blackberry vines tolerate partial shade, but full sun will help the vines produce the best harvest. Take care not to plant blackberries next to tomatoes, wild blackberries, strawberries, or peppers; these plants are vulnerable to the same pests and diseases as blackberries. In warmer areas, blackberries can be planted anytime from late fall to early spring. In colder areas, spring is a best time to plant.

Keep blackberry roots moist while planting. Erect varieties can be planted 3-4 feet apart. Trailing and semi-erect varieties should be planted about 5 feet apart. Space rows 6-10 feet apart. Once plants are covered, water each plant thoroughly. Blackberries are shallow-rooted, so they should be watered frequently in hot, dry weather. The soil around blackberry plants should not become dry to a depth of 6 inches during the growing season. Keep the top inch of soil moist during first 2-3 weeks after planting. Water during the day when possible to minimize any potential disease issues.

## Pollination

Many blackberries are self-fertile and will produce berries on their own without another plant for pollination. But for best production, plant at least two varieties of blackberries. The added pollen from another blackberry variety will enhance blackberry production on all vines.

## Cultivation

Blackberry plants benefit from a layer of mulch to help maintain soil moisture and control weeds. Ensure the plants receive 1-2 inches of water per week during the growing season, either from rain or watering. During the last few weeks of berry production, increase irrigation to 4 inches per week. Lightly fertilize with a 10-10-10 fertilizer or an organic equivalent during the first year. In the second year, fertilize a little more heavily. Spread fertilizer a few inches away from the stems to avoid burning the roots.

A blackberry flower in spring

## Pruning

Blackberries produce fruit on two year-old canes. After the berries are harvested, prune these canes to the ground and either burn them or disposed of them offsite. On new canes, top the vines at 36-48 inches tall. This encourages lateral branching and increases cane strength. Remove damaged or weak canes, and cut out any canes that are closer than 6 inches to another cane. Dispose of any pruned vines to prevent the spread of disease.

## Container Growing

Blackberries are readily grown in containers. They grow best in any container that is 5 gallons or larger. The best containers are wider than they are deep to allow the shallow blackberry roots to expand sideways rather than down. Larger containers allow for the development of more canes, which increases berry yield. All containers should have holes in the bottom for drainage. For the first year, the potting mix will provide the necessary nutrients; additional fertilizer will be needed in early spring each subsequent year. Containerized plants will need to be watered as often as every day during the hottest part of summer. Plants are more susceptible to cold

temperatures in containers, so growers in colder areas should move the blackberry plants to a protected area in winter. Natchez, Arapaho, and Ouachita are all good blackberry cultivars for container growing.

**Propagation**

The most common ways to propagate blackberries are stem and root cuttings. To propagate by stem cuttings, remove a 6 inch stem section from an old primocane in late fall/early winter. The stem cutting can be dipped in rooting hormone and place in a moist medium, such as a seed starting mix or a blend of perlite and peat moss. After 3-4 weeks, roots will develop in a greenhouse setting.

Ripe and unripe blackberries

Root cuttings are taken in winter when the blackberry plant is dormant. Take 3-6 inch cuttings from the roots of healthy blackberry plants and bundle them together in mulch or soil outside while it's cold. After about a month, place these root cuttings a half inch deep in a mix of sand and peat moss, spacing them 2-3 inches apart. Cover the cutting containers in clear plastic; they should sprout in spring.

Air layering is an easy blackberry propagation method. To air layer, gently pull a primocane to the ground and bury the end during the fall. It will sprout roots by spring, when it can be cut from the vine. Air layering done in the summer will produce roots by fall, at which time it can be cut from the plant and transplanted.

**Harvesting**

Depending on the area, blackberries ripen from late spring to early fall. The peak season is usually from July to August. Pick blackberries 1 to 2 days after they become shiny and black, ensuring peak sweetness. Ripe berries will show little resistance when gently pulled off. Be careful of thorns when harvesting berries from thorny varieties. Berries should be picked on cool, dry mornings to extend shelf life, Do not wash berries until ready to use. Blackberry juice will stain anything it touches.

A freshly harvested blackberry

# CHAPTER 1
# BLACKBERRY

# CHAPTER 2
# CURRANTS

# CURRANTS

Currants (*Ribes* sp.) are a species of bush that produce a small, juicy fruit. They are commonly used in landscaping thanks to their delicate appearance and aesthetic appeal. They produce a delicious edible currant. Currant plants require little maintenance, making them an ideal plant for the lazy gardener.

The name *currant* dates back to the time of the ancient Greeks and is a mistranslation of a Greek word for raisin. There are three general types of currants:

- **Redcurrant**: Native to Western Europe, the redcurrant (*Ribes rubrum* and others) produces a somewhat tart red berry on an attractive shrub. Other redcurrant species are native to northern Asia (*R. spicatum*) and North America (*R. triste*). Redcurrant bushes are easy and low maintenance. There are a number of named varieties available in the nursery trade. Redcurrants have been consumed by humans in Europe, North America, and Asia for centuries.

- **White currant**: Though actually an albino form of *Ribes rubrum*, white currants are smaller and sweeter than redcurrants. The white currant is a beautiful plant that is often planted strictly for ornamental purposes. They grow best in areas with cooler climates.

- **Blackcurrant**: *Ribes nigrum* is native to Europe and Asia and is widely grown in temperate regions around the world. There are many cultivars of blackcurrant; they've been cultivated for over 1000 years. Blackcurrant serves as a vector of certain diseases that impact currants and other plants. It is a host of white pine blister rust, a fungal disease impacting pine trees. For

this reason, blackcurrant was banned across the United States for several decades. Bans in some states remain on the books; check state laws before planting. Blackcurrant is more susceptible to disease and pests than any other type of currant, though it grows over a much wider geographic area. Blackcurrants have a unique flavor that is off-putting to some people.

European settlers brought a variety of currants to North America. Native Americans had already been cultivating *R. triste* and eating the wild currants for centuries before European contact. Currants of all types are high in vitamins C, B1, B5, and B6, as well as iron, fiber, calcium, phosphorus, and copper. Redcurrants have been used as a skin rejuvenating face mask. All currants are relatively easy to grow, producing fruit with minimal effort.

## Care and Cultivation

### Site Selection and Soil

Currants grow well in almost any soil type. Blackcurrants in particular are tolerant of even heavy clay soils; white currants will grow in any soil type as long as the soil pH is neutral to slightly acidic. All currants grow and produce well in full sun or partial shade. In warmer areas, such as the southern U.S., currants will grow best in partial shade.

To plant currants, space holes 3- 4 feet apart, and if planting in rows, space rows about 6 feet apart. Care should be taken when planting; the roots are fine and can be damaged easily. Gently fill in hole with soil around the currant plants and water them in. Don't soak the soil and leave standing water; just ensure that the soil is thoroughly moistened.

### Pollination

Currants are technically self-pollinating, but they produce more fruit if other varieties of currants are in the vicinity.

### Cultivation

Currant plants should have 1- 2 inches of water per week from either rainfall or irrigation, especially when fruiting. Any dead or broken branches, or branches

making contact with the ground, should be pruned and discarded. In late winter (or early spring in colder areas), currant bushes should be pruned. Do not prune any branches – except diseased branches – after the first year of growth. In the second winter (or early spring), prune currant plants so that 3 or 4 of both new and two year old branches remain. Canes that are 4 to 5 years or older can be removed to make room for more productive, younger canes, though many varieties will produce on older canes. Black currants should be pruned so that canes no older than two years remain on the plant.

Currant plants benefit from a 2-4 inch layer of mulch to retain moisture and control weeds. After the first year, fertilize currant plants in spring with a balanced fertilizer, such as 10-10-10 or a blend of organic compost and manure.

Redcurrants

## Container Growing

Due to their small size, currants can easily be grown in containers. They do best in any container that's at least 2 feet wide and 20 inches deep. The bottom of the container should have plenty of holes for good drainage, and should be lined with rocks. The plant should be repotted with new soil every 4-5 years to keep it healthy. Place the container in full sun or partial shade and fertilize every spring.

## Pests and Diseases

Redcurrant and white currant have few disease or pest issues, beyond the occasional typical garden pest. Blackcurrant, however, is impacted by a number of diseases. White pine rust, the disease that triggered the ban in the U.S., can harm the plant, though it can also harm other currants as well. Fruit production isn't harmed by white pine rust, but the plant can be slow to recover from it. Other diseases, such as powdery mildew, can be controlled by fungicides if fruit production is impacted.

White currants

### Enjoying The Harvest

Blackberries can be frozen for up to 6 months in freezer bags. They can also be dried in the oven or in a food dehydrator. They can be canned or made into jellies, jams, wine, or pies. For a tasty and easy blackberry cobbler, try this recipe:

## BLACKBERRY COBBLER

**What do you need:**
- ☑ 1 cup self-rising flour
- ☑ 1 cup sugar
- ☑ 1 cup milk
- ☑ 1 stick of butter
- ☑ 1 ½ cups fresh blackberries

**How to prepare it?**

1. Preheat oven to 375°F

2. Melt butter and pour into an 8 x 8 inch baking dish.

3. Mix together flour, sugar and milk. Pour over the melted butter in the baking dish. Place the blackberries on the flour mixture starting in the middle of the batter. (The fruit will spread out when the flour rises up and over it).

4. Bake for approximately 45 to 55 minutes or until it turns golden brown.

5. Serve with vanilla ice cream or whip cream.

Redcurrants, white currants, and blackcurrants

Several insects are attracted to blackcurrant plants. Regular spraying of the plants with insecticidal soap, usually every 7 days, will help reduce the impacts of insect pests.

**Propagation**

Currants are easily propagated by cuttings. When bushes are pruned in the winter or early spring, the pruned stems can be used for propagation. Cut the pruned stems to about 12 inches in length. Strip the leaves off the bottom six inches to encourage root growth. A rooting hormone can be used to increase chances of success, though this is not necessary for successful rooting. Snip the tip of the cutting to encourage it to branch out when it sprouts. Keep the soil moist but not wet as the cuttings root and keep the cuttings out of direct sunlight. Currants can be rooted in pots, or directly in the ground where desired. They will root in 1-2 months, depending on the climate.

### Harvesting

Currants are ripe at different times throughout the summer and early fall, depending on the type of currant and the variety. Each type of currant has a distinct color; once the fruit reaches that color, then it's time to taste test a currant or two to check for ripeness. Currants can be picked individually or as a whole group if all have ripened on a plant. No special tools are needed for harvesting currants. Redcurrants and white currants are sweet and juicy at harvest, while blackcurrants will have a unique, sweet berry flavor. Blackcurrants will be so dark purple that they appear almost black when ripe.

## Enjoying The Harvest

Red and white currants are tasty and can be eaten fresh from the bush. They can also be made into jams, jellies, pies, and preserves. They can even be used whole in muffins and bread.

Currants of all types can be frozen on the stems and then placed into plastic freezer bags. Frozen currants will keep for a year.

Currants can be air-dried or dried in a food dehydrator. They will keep fresh for a couple of weeks in the refrigerator.

Blackcurrants can be juiced and made into a syrup, jelly, or wine. They can also be eaten fresh, though for some people they are an acquired taste. Blackcurrant pies or pudding are a tasty regional dessert in some parts of the world. Currants are naturally high in pectin, which means that they can often be used for jams and jellies without the addition of commercial pectin.

Try this recipe for a simple currant jam (made with any type of currant):

## CURRANT JAM

**What do you need:**
- ☑ 1 quart washed currants
- ☑ 2 and ¼ cups sugar
- ☑ ¼ cup water

**How to prepare it?**

1. Smash currants in a pot with a potato masher or bottle bottom.

2. Add the water to the pot and slowly stir into mashed currants.

3. Stir in sugar and heat mixture on a medium heat. Stir constantly until sugar is dissolved. Once the sugar is dissolved, raise the heat to high and bring the mixture to a boil, stirring constantly.

4. When the mixture starts to congeal (usually 5 minutes or less), remove from heat and place in sterile canning jars. Seal jars according to manufacturer's recommendation.

# CHAPTER 3
# ELDERBERRY

# ELDERBERRY

Elderberry (*Sambucus* sp) is a widely distributed hardwood tree that grows in temperate and subtropical regions of the world. Dozens of different species grow across the world. In North America, *Sambucus canadensis* is the most common species, ranging from the eastern half of Canada down through central Texas.

The blue and purple elderberries are edible and have been used for centuries by people throughout the world. The berries are high in Vitamin C and are edible fresh from the tree. They can also be made into jams, jellies, pies, and wines. The wood of the elderberry tree has a soft pithy center, which means it's easily hollowed out. It was traditionally used for flutes and blowguns. The younger stems and twigs were used as arrow shafts by some Native American tribes.

Virtually all parts of the elderberry have been used medicinally in traditional medicine. The flowers and berries in particular are loaded with antioxidants. Bears, deer, birds, and small rodents all browse the leaves, flowers, and berries of the elderberry. The tree is fast growing and produces berries while young, often producing fruit at 2-3 years of age and reaching mature height in as little as 3-4 years.

Even the flowers of the elderberry are useful. A tea made from elderberry flowers has been reported to do everything from boosting the immune system to reducing indigestion.

In North America, there is a small amount of commercial production of elderberries in Oregon. Besides fruit production, the trees are also planted to control erosion on some sites due to their tolerance of poor soils. There are a few elderberry cultivars that have recently entered the nursery trade.

Some people report nausea when eating more than a handful of raw elderberries due to certain chemical compounds found in the raw berries. Care should be taken when consuming raw elderberry; cooking, boiling, and otherwise processing elderberries for wine, jam, pies, or other uses will break down these compounds, reducing the chance of any ill effects.

## Care and Cultivation

### Site Selection and Soil

Elderberry grows best in well-drained, slightly acidic soil, though the tree will grow well enough in any well-drained soil. Elderberry trees can tolerate wet, slow-draining soils, though growth and production will be limited. The trees can grow in partial shade to full sun locations. They will grow in partial sun in the understory of larger trees.

If the proper elder species is selected, such as *Sambucus canadensis* in most of North America, the plants require little additional care.

Elderberry plants

## Pollination

Elderberry trees are partially self-fertile, which means they will bear a crop of berries on their own, but they produce a larger crop in the presence of another tree. This usually means planting at least two named varieties, or at least two wild trees to ensure maximum berry yield.

Elderberry flowers

## Cultivation

If planted in rich soil in a sunny area, elderberry trees require very little care. They do require water during dry spells, especially while young. A mature elderberry tree is fairly drought tolerant, though supplemental water will help it produce berries during droughts. The tree requires no special pruning, though the gardener can prune off dead or diseased branches. An application of mulch around elderberry trees helps maintain soil moisture and reduces weed competition. Plant elderberry trees at least 6-10 feet apart.

Native elderberry trees need only minimal supplemental fertilization. For maximum berry production, apply rich compost in spring and summer. For commercial fertilizer, use ½ pound of 10-10-10 per year of age for each elderberry tree. Up to 4 pounds of fertilizer can be used on mature trees.

## Container Growing

The elderberry tree is a vigorous tree but it can be grown in containers. The container size should be upgraded at regular intervals to accommodate the growing roots. Use well-drained potting soil and place the tree in full or partial sun.

## Pests and Diseases

When grown in a permaculture setting or when just a few trees are grown, elderberry trees suffer from few pests. Most pests for elderberries are typical garden pests – thrips, aphids, various other pests that are usually easily controlled with insecticidal soap.

## Propagation

Elderberry trees are fairly easy to propagate. They can be propagated by stem cutting, root cutting, or seed. Propagation by seed is useful for propagating native plants, though the trees will be of various vigor and quality due to genetic variability.

The home gardener can easily take hardwood or softwood stem cuttings. Hardwood cuttings are taken from dormant growth, usually in late fall through early spring. Take 6-10" cuttings off branches that are pencil-width and larger, making sure to have several buds per cutting. Place these hardwood cuttings directly in the soil outside. Rooting success by this method varies, but rooting hormone or willow water helps increase the number of successfully rooted cuttings.

Softwood cuttings are taken from the current year's growth, from spring through mid-summer. Take 3-6" cuttings of stems that are pencil-width or slightly smaller. Dip the end in rooting hormone and place the cutting in a well-drained, clean medium, such as a blend of 50% perlite and 50% peat moss. Place cuttings into this mix about an inch deep and then place containers with cuttings into a greenhouse, or drape

with a plastic bag out of direct sunlight. The new roots should emerge in 3-4 weeks. Keep the soil mixture moist but not soaked.

Elderberry can also be propagated by root cuttings. Cut off a piece of root from mature, healthy elderberry trees in winter, removing the roots in 6 inch sections. Pencil width sections are ideal. Plant these root cuttings in the desired location outside. They should start sprouting in late spring.

**Harvesting**

Harvest elderberries from mid-August to mid-September, depending on the climate and region where the trees are grown. The entire "head" of elderberries is normally

Ripe elderberry cluster

harvested, since each flower cluster produces berries that ripen about the same time. The berries are dark purple – almost black – when ripe. Remove the berries once the majority of the berries in the cluster are dark purple. The berries on a particular plant will usually ripen over 1-2 weeks.

The cluster of berries can now be cut up into the individual stems that make up the cluster With the berries still attached to the stem, rinse each cluster of berries under cold water. The elderberries can be pulled off individually, or a fork can be used to quickly removed berries from the stems over a large bowl. Throw out any unripe berries.

Fresh elderberries can also be frozen on the stems and then the frozen berries can be snapped off one at a time.

## Enjoying The Harvest

Elderberries don't keep for long – which is why they are so seldom sold fresh in stores or farmers' markets. They can be dried in food dehydrators or simply air-dried in a sunny location on a hot, dry day. They can also be frozen with the stems attached. To freeze elderberries, place clean berries that have been patted dry into freezer bags. Frozen elderberries should keep for about a year.

Elderberries make excellent wine, jams, jellies, and pies.

For a simple elderberry jelly, try this recipe:

# ELDERBERRY JELLY

**What do you need:**
- ☑ 3 c. elderberry juice (prepared from elderberries juiced through cheesecloth)
- ☑ ¼ c lemon juice
- ☑ 1 pkt Sure Jell (or other pectin)
- ☑ 4 ½ c. Sugar

**How to prepare it?**

1. Add elderberry juice, lemon juice, and pectin to pot and bring to a boil on high heat. Add sugar to the mixture, stirring constantly. Lower heat slightly and watch for the foam! Lower the heat if it's boiling over. Continue stirring.

2. When the juice, pectin, and sugar mixture is boiling so hard that it cannot not be diminished with stirring, stop stirring and set timer for 2 minutes.

3. At exactly two minutes, pour the mixture into prepared jelly jars. Place canning car lids on jars while still hot. Seal jars according to manufacturer's recommendations.

4. Elderberry has retained a reputation for boosting the immune system, especially as it relates to flu and other viruses. A simple immune system booster can be made from a mixture of one part elderberry juice, one part honey, and a little clean water.

# CHAPTER 4
# FIG

# FIG

Figs (*Ficus carica*) have been part of human history from the beginning (Genesis 3:7). A 2006 article in the journal *Science* described fig trees as the oldest fruit cultivated by man, with archeological evidence indicating fig tree cultivation in the Middle East starting around 11,000 years ago.

Fig tree cultivars were brought to North America by settlers from the Mediterranean regions of Europe, primarily Spain and France. By the 1800s, the fig was common at virtually every home across the southern half of United States. One writer, an entomologist named L.O. Howard, noted that fresh figs were served with sugar and cream during the summer months in the much of the United States.

Today, virtually all the commercial production of figs in the United States is in California, though there are some orchards experimenting with commercial fig production in Texas. Almost 40,000 tons of figs are produced annually in California. Of these, 90% are processed for food products

The southern half of the United States, Central America, the Mediterranean regions of Europe, and much of Africa and South Asia are ideal fig growing regions. Most fig varieties are sensitive to cold, but the relatively mild winters in these regions allow fig trees to grow much as they do in the tropics. Gardeners in more northern latitudes must protect figs from severe cold, while mature fig trees in these regions require little or no cold protection once established.

Though considered a fruit tree, figs themselves are not technically a fruit—they are a hollow stem containing flowers and undeveloped fruit. There are a few different types of figs, but only the common fig (*Ficus carica*) does well in temperate regions.

In the tropics, fig trees can grow as tall as 50 feet. In the temperate regions of the world, they most commonly grow to 20-25 feet due to periodic dieback of branches caused by occasional cold weather.

## Care and Cultivation

### Site Selection and Soil

Unlike most other cultivated fruit trees, fig trees do well in almost any soil type, including heavy clay soils, though they tend to do best in loam soils. In sandy soils, fig trees can be harmed by root-knot nematodes.

Fig trees need full sun for optimal growth and production. In cooler areas, it is a good idea to plant fig trees on the south side of a building or structure to protect the tree from cold winter winds.

Ripening figs

A ripe fig

## Pollination

Common fig trees – the figs that do well in the much of the temperate regions of the world - do not require pollination to set fruit.

## Cultivation

Of all the cultivated, non-native fruit trees grown in the temperate regions, fig trees are the easiest to grow. There is no need to thin the figs as they grow, though figs should be picked as soon as they are ripe. Ripe figs have a distinct color and are soft to the touch—they seem to separate effortlessly from the tree. Figs stop ripening as soon as they are picked, so green figs, if harvested, will not ripen further.

In many areas, birds and other animals compete with people for figs. Bird netting, scarecrows, and even clanging aluminum pie plates have all been used with varying degrees of success to keep birds away from figs. To ensure a maximum harvest, pick figs at least once a day when they are ripening.

Fig trees will grow to a height of 15-20 feet, with a 20 foot spread, so fig trees should be spaced 20-25 feet apart at planting, unless they will be intensely pruned during cultivation.

It is always best to fertilize based on a soil test. In rich organic soil, fig trees may go years without requiring fertilizer, though a small amount of annual fertilization is recommended. It is best to use an organic fertilizer or a conventional fertilizer like 10-10-10 or 8-8-8; avoid any fertilizer that is high in nitrogen, as this can lead to disease and low fruit production. Fertilize figs trees lightly, adding a layer of compost an inch or two from the trunk or a few cups of conventional fertilizer in the drip zone beneath the tree's branches. Fig trees grown in sandy soil may need more nutrients than trees grown in other soil types.

**Pruning**

Most of the time, fig trees do not need pruning. In most cases, they will grow into multi-trunk trees. Prune off any diseased or rotting trunks to prolong the life of the tree.

## Container Growing

Fig trees grow large, but can be pruned with few issues for the tree. For this reason, almost any fig variety can be container-grown, if the gardener is prepared to keep it pruned and to keep it watered, especially on hot summer days. The container will have to be increased in size at regular intervals, since fig trees are fast-growing. Use a well-draining potting soil mix and fertilize the containerized fig tree each spring.

## Pests and Diseases

Compared to most other cultivated fruit trees, figs are relatively pest and disease free. Here are a few pests and diseases that can cause problems with fig trees:

### *Fig Rust*

Fig rust is a fungal disease that can be an issue in the humid regions. In years with heavy rain during the growing season, fig rust causes the leaves to turn brown and fall off, reducing plant vigor and fruit yield. Copper spray is effective at controlling this disease, but only if it is applied as soon as possible after the rust appears.

### *Root-Knot Nematodes*

Root-knot nematodes are native microscopic organisms that feed on tissue in plant roots. They can impact fig trees, causing a decline in plant vigor and eventually tree death. There is no cure for root-knot nematodes, but fig trees planted in sandy soil are very susceptible to them. If possible, plant fig trees in loam or even clay soil to prevent attacks of root-knot nematode.

### *Fig Tree Mosaic Virus*

This viral disease has no cure and is thought to come from California, where it sometimes causes damage to the commercial fig crop. Fig trees infected with mosaic virus have deformed fruit and mottled leaves. The virus is within the tissue and will ultimately kill the tree. Fig stock from reputable nurseries should be virus-free.

## Propagation

Fig trees are easy to propagate by a number of methods. Hardwood cuttings, taken in late winter just before the buds break, can be directly planted in the field. Take cuttings that are 8-12 inches long from healthy branches. Remove the cuttings with an angled cut to help seal the fig tree tissue from disease. Place the cuttings 2-3 inches deep in native soil or in containers in a sunny location outdoors. The cuttings should sprout in late spring; the use of rooting hormone will increase the chance of successful cuttings.

Fig trees can also be layered, a process they may do naturally on their own. To layer a fig tree, bend a supple branch to the ground, removing any leaves that remain on the nodes near the soil. Bury the branch at the point it touches the soil, placing a rock or soil-filled container on the location to keep the branch down. The layered branch will root in the soil and can be cut and transplanted during the following dormant season.

**Harvesting**

Fig trees begin production at a very young age. They usually begin producing during the first year of growth or soon thereafter. Maximum production begins when the trees are 5-7 years old and will continue for decades. Harvest figs when they are the ripe color for their cultivar (often dark brown, but sometimes purple or green). The fig should pull from the tree with a gentle tug.

## Enjoying The Harvest

Figs have been preserved in many ways over the millennia. In the southern U.S., fig preserves are a traditional favorite, along with fig jam. Figs are used in countless dishes across the world.

Figs can also be dried in the oven or a food dehydrator. To oven-dry figs, cut them in half and place them on an ungreased cookie sheet with the cut part facing up. Turn the oven on low and leave the oven door cracked a little if possible. In 12 hours, the figs will be dried. In areas with lower humidity, fig trees can be sun-dried on a sunny day. They should last several weeks at room temperature.

To make some tasty fig preserves, try the recipe listed here:

http://southernfood.about.com/od/datesandfigs/r/blbb424.htm

For a unique take on pinwheel pastries, try this recipe:

## PINWHEEL PASTRIES

**What do you need:**
- ☑ One sheet thawed pastry dough
- ☑ 6 Whole sliced figs
- ☑ 2 tablespoons honey
- ☑ a few dashes of nutmeg and cinnamon
- ☑ 1 tablespoon butter

**How to prepare it?**

1. Pre-heat oven to 375°F
2. Roll out pastry dough thin and place on a parchment lined baking sheet pan and bake for 4-5 minutes (keep it pliable)
3. In a sauce pan add butter, fig slices, cinnamon, nutmeg, honey and cook 15 minutes or until fruit is tender, Place in a mixing bowl and stir well to a consistency to spread on top of pastry dough
4. Roll pastry filled dough up and place back on baking sheet pan, bake additional 6 minutes or until golden brown
5. Allow to cool slightly before slicing
6. Serve warm

# CHAPTER 5
# GOUMI BERRY

# GOUMI BERRY

Goumi (*Elaeagnus multiflora*) is a shrub that produces small, edible berries with little effort on the gardener's part. Native to parts of Asia, goumi berries were historically used for both food and medicine. In addition to producing edible, nutritious berries, the plant also fixes atmospheric nitrogen into the soil around the roots, thanks to a symbiotic relationship it shares with certain bacteria species. Goumi berries are often called cherry silverberries.

Goumi grows into a small tree of about 20 feet if left unpruned. It can be pruned into a hedge and used in a landscape planting, or it can be grown mixed with other perennial fruit and berry plants to reduce the need for nitrogen fertilizer in the garden or orchard.

In their native range, goumi berries have been part of the traditional diet for centuries. They are rich in vitamins, with a sweet and tangy flavor, making them perfect for fresh eating, jam, or pies. They contain more lycopene than tomatoes.

The plants are so easy to grow that in tropical and subtropical climates they can become naturalized. Their ability to fix nitrogen allows them to grow in poorer soils and still generate adequate growth for fruit production. Goumi itself is not an invasive species, though some other plants of the genus *Elaeagnus* can become invasive in certain climates.

Goumi is either deciduous or evergreen, depending on the climate. The fruit contains a single seed and most goumi plants have thorns on them. The plant has fine silver scales covering the leaves, making goumi an attractive edible landscape plant.

It blooms in the spring with small fragrant flowers, producing one crop of berries per year, usually in mid-summer.

There are a few named varieties of goumi berries, with Sweet Scarlet and Red Gem being the most commonly-available in the nursery trade. Goumi grows and produces in cold winter areas, subtropical areas, and all climates in between. The plants are fast-growing and they begin producing a crop at 2-3 years of age. Goumi berry plants are hardy to -25°F!

## Care and Cultivation

### Site Selection and Soil

Goumi plants thrive in virtually all soil conditions, with the exception of extremely wet soils. They require at least six hours of direct sunlight per day for best production. They can tolerate some shade and still produce a crop of berries.

### Pollination

Goumi is partially self-fertile but will produce a better crop of berries with two different plants.

### Cultivation

Goumi can be pruned to any size or allowed to grow into a small tree, depending on the specific situation where it is grown. Since it is a nitrogen-fixing plant, Goumi will provide some plant-available nitrogen to nearby plants. It fits in well as part of a permaculture system.

Keep the plant watered during dry periods for the first year or two after planting; after that, goumi is drought resistant. Supplemental watering during droughts will help the goumi plant produce more fruit.

The area around a young goumi plant should be weeded and mulched for best growth during the first couple of years. Since they manufacture their own nitrogen, goumi berries need very little supplemental fertilizer. Applications of compost or composted manure once or twice a year may increase berry yields.

**Container Growing**

Due to their good-natured attitude about pruning, goumi berries lend themselves to being cultivated in a container garden. Plant goumi berry plants in well-drained potting mix and place the container in an area with at least 6 hours of sunlight per day. Keep the plant pruned so that it doesn't outgrow the pot; if it does, transfer it to a slightly larger container, lightly trimming the roots prior replanting.

**Pests and Diseases**

Goumi plants are not typically harmed by any major pests or diseases. Any garden pest that does harm them can be controlled using insecticidal soap.

**Propagation**

Goumi can be propagated by seed, but it is a difficult process. The seeds should be planted one inch deep in fertile soil in later summer; it will take at least 18 months for the seedlings to emerge!

A faster propagation method involves taking cuttings of the goumi plant. Hardwood cuttings taken from an existing plant and stuck into a container with well-drained soil or into the ground should root in about a year.

Softwood cuttings, taken from the current season's growth (usually in July or August), can be placed in a mixture of peat moss and perlite (or sand and perlite) in a humid environment, such as under mist in a greenhouse or in a large closed plastic bag. Take six inch cuttings and remove the lower leaves. Dip the cuttings in rooting hormone and place at least an inch of the stem into the perlite or other propagation

mix. Rooting times vary, but it is much easier and faster to create new plants with this method.

**Harvesting**

Goumi berries are ripe in mid-summer, usually in July. They are bright red when ripe. Unripe berries are much more sour than sweet. Unripe berries can be used in jams and pies; they can even be substituted for gooseberries in recipes.

Fully ripe berries should come off the plant with a quick tug. They taste sweet, with a moderate amount of juice. Typical yield for a mature goumi plant is 15-20 pounds of berries.

Harvested goumi berries

## Enjoying The Harvest

Ripe goumi berries are tasty right off the bush, with no preparation. They can also be dried on a food dehydrator or in the sun. To dry goumi berries, slice them in half and remove the seeds and stem and place them in a food dehydrator or in direct sunlight on a dry day. Fully dried goumi berries can be kept in sealed containers for several months. Fresh goumi berries will keep for a week or two in the refrigerator.

Goumi berries can also be frozen. To freeze the berries, slice them in half and remove the seeds and stem. Put the sliced berries in freezer bags and place in the freezer. Frozen goumi berries will keep for about a year.

For an easy and tasty goumi jelly recipe, try this recipe.

## GOUMI JELLY

**What do you need:**
- ☑ 6 pints of sliced goumi berries with seeds removed
- ☑ ½ cup of water
- ☑ 1 and ½ cup of sugar
- ☑ 1 box of pectin

**How to prepare it?**

1. Simmer berries in water for about 10 minutes.

2. Pour berries and water through cheese cloth. This should yield about 3 and ½ or 4 cups of juice.

3. Mix ¼ cup of sugar with the pectin, then add this to the goumi juice in a sauce pan. Slowly add the remaining sugar, stirring continually.

4. Bring the mixture to a rolling boil. Let boil for 5 minutes, stirring constantly. After 5 minutes, remove from heat and skim off the foam.

5. Pour into jars and seal with lids according to the manufacturer's recommendation.

# CHAPTER 6
# HONEYBERRY

# HONEYBERRY

Honeyberry (*Lonicera caerulea*) is a non-invasive relative of the common Japanese honeysuckle. Native to various locations in the Northern Hemisphere, honeyberry (also called haskap) underwent extensive hybridization in Russia and Japan in the 20th century.

Honeyberry was first officially documented in 1755. Researchers found that this berry had been used in northern Japan and Siberia for centuries. The plant itself is a medium-sized bush that grows to 3-8 feet in height. Thanks to the decades of breeding, there are now dozens of honeyberry varieties.

The honeyberries themselves are elongated and blue, growing after a flush of beautiful white flowers that resemble Japanese honeysuckle flowers. The berries are ripe from late spring to mid-summer, depending on the variety. Honeyberries are hardy to -55°F! Honeyberry bushes grow well as far south as the southern end of USDA zone 8 and similar climates around the world.

Honeyberries make attractive landscape plants, though they are usually grown just for their berries. The honeyberry is grown extensively as a garden plant outside of North America; it is just now becoming more commonly available in the U.S. There is commercial production of honeyberries in several countries.

Honeyberries are rich in nutrients, including Vitamin C and other antioxidants. They also taste great and require minimal care. The honeyberry is disease and pest resistant, making it ideal for organic gardening.

## Care and Cultivation

**Site Selection and Soil**

Honeyberries grow best in moist, well-drained soil, though they are tolerant of slower-draining clay soils. They are also tolerant of a wide range of soil pH levels (4.5-8.5). In northern latitudes, honeyberry bushes should be planted in full sun; in the southern U.S. and similar climates around the world, they should be planted in a location that gets afternoon shade. When planting, holes should be wide enough to allow the roots to spread out completely. The plants can be spaced 3-6 feet apart.

**Pollination**

Honeyberry plants require two varieties for pollination purposes. Select two varieties that bloom at the same time to ensure compatible pollination. Honeyberries are pollinated by bees and native pollinators, including bumble bees. Better pollination is achieved with plants spaced no more than 6 feet apart.

Honeyberry blooms look similar to Japanese honeysuckle

Ripe honeyberries

## Cultivation

Honeyberry plants love to be mulched. An organic mulch 2-4 inches thick is optimal for retaining soil moisture and discouraging weed growth. Honeyberries are naturally shallow-rooted, which means that they are sensitive to drought and even short dry spells. The plants should be watered regularly during the first year. In subsequent years, the plants should be watered during any dry spell and the soil should stay moist (not saturated) during berry production.

Honeyberry plants can be planted in the fall and winter in the southern U.S. and similar climates. It's best to wait until early spring to plant them in areas with colder winters and frozen soils.

Fertilize honeyberry plants once in the spring using rich organic compost, complete organic fertilizer, or a balanced commercial fertilizer, such as 12-12-12.

Honeyberry (haskap) blooms

## Container Growing

Honeyberry plants are compact enough in size that container growing is possible. Plant honeyberries in containers in early spring, using a container large enough to accommodate all the roots, with space to grow.

Use a well-draining potting soil mix and line the bottom of the container with rocks to improve drainage.

## Pests and Diseases

Honeyberry plants do not have any significant pest or disease issues. They are usually only bothered by minor garden pests that can be easily controlled with insecticidal soap if they begin to seriously harm the plant.

Honeyberry plants are beloved by birds and other wildlife; bird netting may be necessary in some cases to protect the ripening berries from hungry airborne scavengers.

## Propagation

Honeyberry is a relatively easy plant to propagate by cutting. Take 6-12 inch cuttings of dormant stems anytime from late fall to late spring. Place the cuttings in a suitable propagation media, such as a blend of peat moss and perlite.

The use of rooting hormone or willow water will increase the number of rooted cuttings but is not necessary. Leave cuttings in a shady location; many of them will begin to sprout in spring.

Honeyberry can also be propagated by transplanting the root shoots that sprout around the plants during the growing season. The best time to move these shoots is when they are dormant – usually winter to early spring.

Honeyberries can also be propagated by air layering. Pull a growing honeyberry branch down towards the ground and remove leaves in a 2-3 inch section of stem. Bury the stem in a pot with soil, using a small stone to keep the branch held down into the pot As the plant grows, the branch will develop roots. By the following spring, the branch can be cut from the main plant and transplanted.

### Harvesting

Honeyberries ripen earlier than many other berries, usually from early May to mid-June. They ripen to a beautiful dark blue color, similar to that of a blueberry. They can be picked individually, or the whole bush can be shaken to make the berries fall on to a tarp or sheet for easier collection. Avoid harvesting unripe berries, because their flavor is tart. Allow the berries to turn dark blue for maximum sweetness.

## Enjoying The Harvest

Ripe honeyberries are tasty right off the plant. They're great on top of salads or yogurt. They can be preserved for a few days in the refrigerator. Honeyberries can also be dried, either on a dry sunny day on screens, or on a food dehydrator. Fully dried honeyberries will last for a few months in sealed containers. Honeyberries can be frozen in freezer bags for up to a year.

Honeyberries can easily be made into jam; this jam can be mixed into a homemade vanilla ice cream recipe to make honeyberry ice cream.

To make honeyberry jam, try this recipe:

## HONEYBERRY JAM

**What do you need:**
- ☑ 4 cups of honeyberries
- ☑ 1 cup sugar
- ☑ 1 tablespoon lemon juice

**How to prepare it?**

1. Mix honeyberries, sugar, and lemon juice in a sauce pan on low-medium heat.

2. Use spoon or potato masher to smash the honeyberries to release their juice.

3. Move heat to medium and continue stirring the mixture until it thickens – this may take as long as 30 minutes. Once it's thickened, remove from heat and add to sterilized jars, or let cool and then use immediately.

4. To make honeyberry ice cream, add ½ to 1 cup of honeyberry jam to the vanilla ice cream mixture, then make ice cream as usual.

# CHAPTER 7
## Japanese (Oriental) PERSIMMON

# Japanese (Oriental) Persimmon

Japanese persimmons (*Diospyros kaki*) are probably one of the oldest plants in continual cultivation, having been cultivated continuously in China for at least the last 2000 years. *Diospyros kaki* trees are called Japanese persimmons or Oriental persimmons in North America; they are native to parts of Japan, China, and Burma. This name is to differentiate them from the smaller-fruited American persimmon that is native to North America. The genus name *Diospyros*, literally means "divine fruit," indicating the persimmon's fame in ancient cultures. It is widely planted in Japan, where it is still an extremely popular fruit.

Marco Polo recorded information about persimmons in China in the 1400s. Japanese persimmons are a relatively new tree in Europe and North America. They were introduced to Europe in the late 1800s. The first persimmon seeds were brought to the United States in the 1850s. Grafted persimmon trees were grown in California in the early 1900s. By the 1920s, persimmons were grown throughout the southeastern United States, where they grew well due to the climate. Today, most commercial production in the United States takes place in California with smaller commercial plantings scattered across the southeastern United States. They are also commercially grown throughout Asia and in some places in Central America.

Oriental persimmon trees are particularly adapted to the heat and humidity. They have very few pests or diseases that harm them and they are one of the longest-living domesticated fruit trees, living and producing fruit for 50 years or more. The trees themselves vary widely in size, growing to 15-30 feet, depending on soil and site conditions.

## Japanese (oriental) Persimmon

Oriental persimmon trees begin bearing fruit when they are three to six years old, depending on the variety. They begin full production when the trees are seven to ten years old. At full production, mature Oriental persimmon trees produce 300-500 pounds of fruit per year.

Many persimmon varieties are astringent, which means that they have a high tannin content that makes them inedible until they are over-ripe. Once these varieties are soft and over-ripe, they are sweet and edible. Other persimmon varieties are non-astringent and can be eaten fresh from the tree. Fuyu is an example of a non-astringent persimmon variety.

Persimmon trees look beautiful in a landscape, with an attractive form and fruit that hangs on the tree well into autumn. The tropical look of the flowers in spring is an added aesthetic benefit. Persimmon wood is extremely hard and is sometimes used for golf clubs and tool handles.

Persimmons in autumn

Young persimmon fruit

## Care and Cultivation

**Site Selection and Soil**

Persimmon trees can reach heights of 25 feet, with a width of nearly the same. They can endure more shade than other fruit trees, though they grow best in full sun. They need at least 6 hours of sunlight during the growing season for optimal fruit production.

Persimmon trees do well in almost any soil type, including clay soil, as long as the soil is well-drained. Persimmons do not grow well in salty soils. The ideal soil pH for persimmon trees is slightly acidic to neutral, usually in a range of 6-7.5.

## Pollination

Oriental persimmons have a unique way of pollinating, with trees producing either male or female flowers. Male flowers pollinate the female flowers thanks to assistance from wind or insects. In commercial orchards, special predominantly-male persimmon varieties are planted among the fruiting persimmon trees to ensure pollination. Self-fertile varieties, such as Fuyu and Izu, bear fruit without another tree for pollination. Most modern cultivars, including the ones listed in this chapter, are self-fertile, so issues with persimmon pollination in the home orchard should be minimal.

## Cultivation

Persimmon trees are delightfully easy to grow. They are often heavy bearers, yielding much more fruit than the tree can easily carry. A heavy crop can lead to limb breakage and biennial bearing. To prevent these issues, persimmon trees should be thinned to a maximum of one fruit every six inches. Thin the fruit about one month after bloom.

Persimmon trees bloom in March and April; the fruit ripens in September, October, and November, depending on the variety. Astringent varieties are traditionally harvested after the first frost, though research indicates that the frost does little to make the fruit sweeter. Persimmons will often hang on the tree after the leaves have fallen, giving a striking and colorful effect to the landscape.

Predation by wildlife can be a major problem with persimmons. Netting, fencing, and decoys can alleviate this problem to some degree. If the problem is major, persimmons that are almost ripe can be harvested and brought inside to ripen.

Oriental persimmon trees are drought tolerant once established, but the trees should be watered every week or ten days during fruit development, whether from rain or irrigation. Regular watering will help the tree yield larger, fuller-flavored fruit. A drip irrigation system or a soaker hose is recommended for persimmon tree

irrigation. Try to prevent the soil from staying waterlogged too long as this can lead to rotten roots.

## Fertilization

In most soils, persimmon trees do not need much fertilizer. Excessive fertilization with nitrogen can cause too much vegetative growth and poor fruit yield. If persimmon trees are planted in a yard, fertilizer leaching from the yard is usually all a persimmon tree needs for fertilization.

If new growth on the tree is less than one foot per year, apply one pound of 10-10-10 fertilizer per inch of tree diameter around the base of the tree (beneath the canopy if the tree is larger.) Organic fertilizers, such as compost or composted manure, can also be used to fertilize persimmon trees if growth is lacking. Apply a layer of organic matter 2-3 inches thick about two inches from the trunk.

## Pruning

Oriental persimmon trees bear fruit on the current season's growth. The trees are pruned into a modified central leader shape, or an open center shape. They can also be pruned short and used as a hedge and they can be topped and kept at whatever height the owner desires. Persimmon trees are also excellent as espalier specimens. Unless there is a diseased branch being removed, prune persimmon trees only in winter.

To prune a persimmon trees into a modified central leader shape, follow these steps:

1. Top the newly planted persimmon tree to a height of 2.5-3 feet above the ground.
2. In the second winter, begin selecting several main branches growing from the trunk of the tree. These branches should be growing vertically. The branches will serve as the scaffold branches for the persimmon tree. Prune off any other vertically-growing branches that will not be used as central leaders.
3. In the third winter, prune off any vertical branches that are crossing or crowding other branches. Leave 3-5 vertical branches growing up from the

trunk. Trim back extremely low growing lateral branches and remove 3-6 inches from lateral branches up the length of the tree.

4. In the fourth and subsequent winters, prune off weak, diseased, or dead wood and any branches that crowd or cross others. The goal is the have about one foot of distance between each of the scaffold branches.

5. After many decades, if the persimmon tree ever seems to be in decline, prune it back severely—this will spur new growth and may save the tree.

## Pests and Diseases

Persimmons are one of the most pest and disease-resistant cultivated fruit trees. Here are a few pests and diseases that can occasionally cause problems on persimmon trees.

### *Bacterial Canker*

Bacterial canker can be a problem in areas where persimmons have been grown for many years in large numbers in intensive culture. The disease enters into fresh wounds in persimmon tree tissue and usually occurs when the weather is warm. The bacteria causes tumor-shaped tissue, called galls, to appear on branches and roots. To control bacterial canker, prune off infected branches as soon as the infection symptoms appear. If the infection persists, it is best to remove and destroy the entire tree.

### *Black Spot*

Black spot is a fungal disease of the leaves and occasionally the fruit. It is usually not economically important unless it impacts the fruit. Only then is fungicide application recommended for commercial orchards. Black spot is not fatal to the tree or fruit.

### *Insect Pests*

Insect pests, such as mealy bugs, aphids, and fruit flies can be a nuisance on some occasions. Insecticidal soap or other pesticides will usually solve the problem if the infestation is severe.

## Container Growing

Persimmon trees that are grafted on dwarf rootstock may be suitable for container growing, though these trees are not readily available in the nursery trade. Certain species of persimmons are occasionally used for bonsai. Standard size persimmon trees are not suitable for container-growing.

## Harvesting

Harvest both astringent and non-astringent persimmons when they are fully colored but hard. This will help prevent loss from wildlife. Remove persimmons from the tree using garden shears, clipping the stem near the top of the fruit. Persimmons will ripen in the refrigerator (where they will stay fresh for up to eight weeks), or at room temperature.

## Enjoying The Harvest

Astringent persimmons, once they are ripe and soft, can be eaten raw; non-astringent persimmon varieties can be eaten while the tissue is hard or after the fruit has been allowed to ripen further and soften. Both types of persimmons will stay fresh in the refrigerator for four to six weeks when fully ripe. Astringent persimmons picked unripe can be frozen overnight to soften the tissue quickly for a sweeter flavor.

Persimmons can also be frozen for preservation. To freeze persimmons, peel and remove any seeds in the persimmon. Puree the fruit using a sieve or food processor and place in freezer bags or containers. To maintain color, add 1/8 teaspoon of ascorbic acid (Vitamin C) to each quart of fruit.

Fuyu persimmons can be cut into slices and peeled while the fruit is ripe but the tissue is still hard. Create a simple syrup of two cups of water and two cups of sugar and heat to boiling in a saucepan. Once the sugar is dissolved, add persimmon slices and bring back to boiling. Allow the persimmon and syrup mixture to cool and then place in freezer bags. Frozen Fuyu persimmon fruit should keep for a year.

Persimmons are traditionally preserved by drying. Any persimmon variety, including the indigenous American persimmon, can be dried. To dry persimmons, peel fully-ripe persimmons and slice the fruit into ¼ inch thick slices. Place in a food

dehydrator for 14 to 18 hours. Once the fruit is dry and brittle, place it into an airtight bag or container. Dried persimmons should keep for at least six months. The dried fruit can be reconstituted in water, or used dried. Persimmons can also be sun-dried when the temperature is over 90 degrees with low humidity.

## Select Persimmon Varieties

Here is a partial list of commonly-available persimmon varieties (all varieties listed need no more than 200 chill hours, and all do well in USDA zones 6-10 and similar climates around the world):

- **Fuyu** - America's favorite persimmon, largely due to the fact that it is non-astringent, which means it can be eaten while the fruit is still firm. The fruit is medium-sized, with deep orange skin. The tree is vigorous and productive, and the fruits keep well. Fuyu is self-fertile, so it does not need a pollinator.

- **Hachiya** - An older variety that is still popular in Japan and the United States. It is grown commercially in California. Hachiya is astringent, but once the fruit is soft, it has a rich, sweet flavor. It is commonly dried and eaten like candy. Hachiya is self-fertile and does not need a pollinator.

- **Eureka** - A heavy-yielding variety that is grown commercially in California and Texas. The fruit is high-quality, astringent, and usually contains seeds. The fruit is medium-sized and oval-shaped, with a reddish-yellow color. It is very sweet and juicy when fully ripe. Eureka is a self-fertile persimmon variety.

- **Tane-Nashi** - Seedless persimmons, with a conical shape and orange color. The tree is moderately productive but vigorous. The tree has a nice branched shape, making it an ideal landscape tree. The persimmons store well and are often dried after harvest. Tane-Nashi is mostly self-fertile, though it produces a larger, sweeter crop when grown near another persimmon tree, such as Fuyu.

- **Suruga** - A non-astringent variety that produces an extremely sweet, high-quality fruit. The fruit keeps well and has a good texture, though it will not soften on the tree. It is a late-ripening variety and the leaves are colorful in autumn. It is self-fertile.

- **Tamopan** - A large persimmon with a unique flat oval shape. The tree is extremely vigorous and moderately productive. Tamopan persimmons have a rich, sweet taste when they are fully ripe. It ripens mid-season and often begins producing at a young age. Tamopan is also self-fertile.

Tamopan persimmon

- **Izu** - A non-astringent persimmon that is more cold-hardy than the Fuyu. It can be eaten straight from the tree. The fruit is large with burnt-orange skin. The tree produces a good crop annually and has good drought tolerance once established. It is an earlier-ripening variety. Izu is self-fertile, so it does not need another variety for pollination.

# CHAPTER 8
# MAHONIA

# MAHONIA

*Mahonia* is a genus of perennial shrubs native to China, North America, and Central America. Cultivation of mahonia for landscape and culinary purposes began in North America in the 1700's. Since then, they've been used across the world as landscape plants. They are generally fuss-free and they make a nice addition to a landscape. They have holly-like leaves with thorns and flowers in late winter when most other garden plants are dormant or just budding out.

Mahonia plants are widely adapted, with specific species being adapted to certain geographic areas. The berries they produce can be eaten fresh or made into jams, jellies, and wines.

Most species of mahonia are evergreen. In late spring into summer, they are covered with purple, yellow, or red berries, depending on the species. All mahonia berries are edible, though the flavor varies between species and even varieties within a species.

---

**Before mahonia berries are eaten, please ensure that the plant is actually mahonia and not holly. Holly berries are toxic to humans if consumed!**

Common mahonia species include the following:

- **Mahonia japonica** – This mahonia species is native to China. It is widely planted across the world as a landscape plant. It produces distinct green leaves, yellow flowers, and small blue or black berries in spring and summer. The berries are tart and seedy, but edible and useful for jams, jellies, and pies.

- **Mahonia aquifolium** – The Oregon grape holly is native to the western United States. It's evergreen, growing to about 3 feet in height. Oregon grape holly has attractive yellow flowers in spring, followed by large clusters of purple or blue berries that resemble grapes. The berries are filled with seeds but tasty. They were part of the diet of several Native American tribes in the Pacific Northwest. The Oregon grape holly is the state flower of Oregon.

- **Mahonia nervosa** – Often called low Oregon grape, nervosa is a smaller mahonia that is native to the western half of North America. The plant is varied in leaf color and a heavy bloomer. The berries that follow the blooms are small, but numerous. The berries are edible and were also used by Native American tribes.

- **Mahonia x media** – This is the most commonly-planted hybrid mahonia species. Several popular varieties of this species are planted in landscapes around the world. The foliage is evergreen, the yellow flowers are attractive, and the berries are plump and numerous. The berries are slightly tart, but with a good flavor. Common varieties of this species include 'Charity', 'Soft Caress', 'Winter Sun', and 'Buckland.' The overall size of *Mahonia x media* depends on the variety. All produce edible berries.

- **Mahonia trifoliolata** – Also called agarita, wild currant, or chaparral berry, this mahonia is about as tough as they come. Native to the arid regions of southwestern North America, *Mahonia trifoliolata* grows best with minimal care. It tolerates extreme heat and drought, and produces small yellow flowers, followed by red berries in April and May. The berries are edible either fresh or preserved. They can be squeezed for juice and used to make wine, or they can be dried and preserved. Berries of agarita were a part of the diet of Native American tribes in the Southwest, including the Apaches and Chihuahuas.

Due to the dozens of species available, a mahonia of some type is suitable for planting across much of the world. Thanks to their resilience and easy nature, they make an ideal part of a lazy gardener's landscape or garden.

Oregon grape holly

## Care and Cultivation

Plant mahonia in either full sun or partial shade. Soil is not an issue for mahonia, provided that the appropriate species is planted in a particular area. Most mahonia cannot tolerate wetland type soils, but slow-draining, clay soils don't cause any issues.

A yearly mulch of compost or other organic material will help ensure that the plant continues to bloom and produce berries. No other supplemental fertilizer is usually necessary, unless the soil is extremely poor.

Mahonia doesn't need pruning, except for the occasional removal of overgrown or old, unproductive stems.

## Container Growing

The typical landscape mahonias, such as *Mahonia x media* or *M. japonica*, are usually tall and not always practical to grow in containers. Other species, such as *M. nervosa*, are more compact and make attractive container plants on their own or with a mix of other perennials.

Plant mahonia in well-drained potting soil. The container should be placed in an area where it gets at least 4-6 hours of sun each day. The containerized mahonia will grow well in all but the deepest shade.

## Pests and Diseases

Insect pests don't usually bother mahonia species, and mahonia-killing diseases are rare. Diseases and insect pests that might attack a mahonia plant don't kill the plant or harm flower or berry production.

Mahonia in bloom

Mahonia flowers

## Propagation

Mahonia can be propagated by seed or by cuttings. To propagate mahonia by seed, collect ripe berries and slice them to remove the seeds. Seeds can be directly planted in the ground once the berries are ripe. Alternatively, the seeds can be placed in moist sand and put in the refrigerator for about 3 months and then planted, either outside or in containers.

Softwood cuttings, taken from the current season's growth, are relatively easy to root in a mix of perlite and peat moss under mist. Hardwood cuttings, taken in winter and planted in either containers or directly in the ground, are sometimes successful.

**Harvesting**

Harvest mahonia berries once they reach their mature color. This color varies by species, but is often dark purple or red. The berries can be harvested individually, which is easier on some species, or the entire spike of berries can be cut from the plant. Most mahonia berries are ripe from May to August.

## Enjoying The Harvest

Mahonia berries can be eaten right off the plant. They can also be air dried or dried on a food dehydrator. They make an excellent, uniquely-flavored jelly.

Ripe mahonia berries

To make mahonia jelly, try this recipe:

## MAHONIA JELLY

**What do you need:**
- ☑ 2-3 cups of mahonia berries
- ☑ 2 cups water
- ☑ 1 ounce of pectin (about half a packet)
- ☑ 2 and ½ cups sugar

**How to prepare it?**

1. Rinse berries and boil mahonia berries in water (2 cups) for 10 minutes.

2. Pour berries and water through a colander over a bowl and use a wooden spoon to smash the pulp and juice through the colander. Throw out the seeds that collect in the colander.

3. Strain the mixture through cheesecloth over the boiling pan. Bring to a boil again and add pectin. Continue boiling and add sugar, stirring constantly.

4. Stir for about 4 minutes total, or until the jelly mixture starts to thicken. Pour into sterile jars and seal tops according to manufacturer's recommendations.

# CHAPTER 9
# MULBERRY

# MULBERRY

Mulberry trees belong to the genus *Morus* and are native to the warm and subtropical regions of North America, Asia, Eurpoe, and Africa. The fruit has been prized since ancient times. The red mulberry (*Morus rubra*) is native to the eastern half of North America, from East Texas to Florida, and up to Canada. The white and black mulberries (*M. alba* and *M. nigra*) are native to Asia and are naturalized in North America, Asia, and to a lesser extent in Europe.

White mulberries will hybridize with native red mulberries, ultimately displacing the native population. Black mulberries have been in cultivation since time immemorial and have been heavily hybridized over millennia. Red and black mulberries are long-lived trees, producing berries over many decades. White mulberries are shorter-lived.

Red mulberries were eaten by American Indians and early settlers. The fruit was eaten raw or dried, and beginning in the nineteenth century, was made into jams, jellies, and mulberry wine. Even childhood rhymes talk about going "'round the mulberry bush." Since mature mulberry trees are tall, fruit was often collected as soon as it fell to the ground. Numerous bird and mammal species consume wild mulberries.

Interestingly, there are a number of non-native mulberry species in the North America. These specimens were imported from Asia in the nineteenth century. They were imported as a food for silk worms during a time when some American entrepreneurs were attempting to establish a silk industry in the United States. Leaves from the white mulberry tree are the only food for certain types of silk worms.

All mulberries are pollinated by wind, which means that some hybridization has taken place between the Asian and American mulberry species. Un-hybridized stands of red mulberries are evident because all berries are a deep red in color, with no white berries or mottled white/red berries. White and black mulberries are cultivated around the world.

## Care and Cultivation

### Site Selection and Soil

While the children's song talks about a bush, mulberry plants actually grow into tall trees. In a native forest setting, the mulberry tree limbs would be quite high, and the mulberries would be consumed as soon as they fell.

Red mulberry

Black mulberry

Mulberry trees of all types need full sun, with space to grow tall. On rich soils, black and red mulberries can grow to almost 70 feet; white mulberries grow to 50-60 feet.

Red and black mulberries will stain (usually temporarily) anything they come in contact with when they fall, including cars, driveways, and roofs. It is generally recommended that they be planted in a location where they will not stain buildings or driveways.

All mulberry trees prefer well-drained, sandy loam soil, and they do not grow well in clay soils. They are tolerant of a wide range of soil pH levels.

Mulberry trees make nice landscape trees, provided they are planted where the berries will not stain anything of importance. Red and black mulberry trees will often live for more than 75 years.

## Pollination

Mulberry trees are pollinated by pollen brought in by wind. Depending on where the tree is planted, there is usually enough mulberry pollen in the air to ensure pollination. To ensure your native mulberries are pollinated by another native tree, plant two native trees in the same general vicinity.

## Cultivation

Mulberry trees are relatively low maintenance. In early spring, be on the look-out for web worms (bag worms, tent caterpillars); they love to infest mulberry trees. These infestations are generally not serious, though if they become serious, it is a good idea to treat the entire tree (if possible) with *Bacillus thoringensis*, an organic pesticide for caterpillars. For safety reasons, it is best not to use fire to eliminate web worms!

Another problem that may occur with mulberry trees is dieback. If part of the tree dies, it is best to prune it off to prevent disease entry into the rest of the tree. This usually involves pruning dead limbs.

Mulberry trees spend their first few years in a bushy stake, usually growing taller and losing their lower limbs after about a decade of growth. They have a relatively quick rate of growth. Mulberry trees generally produce berries while they are still small and bush like, usually after 2-4 years of growth. They will continue to produce for decades.

**Container Growing**

Mulberries of all kinds are vigorous growers; because of this, container growing isn't suitable for many types of mulberries. Dwarf mulberry varieties, including the variety 'Dwarf Everbearing' (a black mulberry), are suitable for containers, where they will produce for years. Any container large enough to accommodate the roots will work. Use a well-drained potting mix and fertilize the tree with a balanced fertilizer each spring.

White mulberry

## Propagation

Native mulberry trees are propagated by seed. Collect seed as soon as possible from ripe berries. Clean seeds gently, then place in cool area for stratification for two to three months. Then plant seeds in spring, in a warm area. Plant no more than ¼ inches deep.

Mulberry trees can also be propagated by cuttings. Small softwood cuttings placed in a humid environment (such as a greenhouse), with adequate moisture (misting) will root. Larger cuttings, when placed in the ground in late winter or spring, and kept moist, will also sometimes be successful.

## Harvesting

Harvest red and black mulberries when they are so dark red that they're almost black. Black mulberries will be the color of blackberries. The native red mulberry will be dark red. Native mulberries may drop from the tree just prior to becoming ripe; these mulberries have a distinct, slightly sour taste but they can be eaten or used in recipes, especially when mixed with ripe mulberries. White mulberries are usually ripe when they fall from the tree.

Red and white mulberries are ripe in late spring and early summer, usually May to June in most climates. Black mulberries are ripe in late summer or early fall.

To harvest mulberries, place a clean sheet on the ground beneath a mulberry tree and shake the tree. The ripe mulberries will fall on the sheet. For larger trees, a ladder may be necessary to reach the limbs. Black mulberries may have to be plucked from the tree by hand.

## Enjoying The Harvest

Mulberries are tasty fresh off the tree. Many people enjoy making mulberry jelly, mulberry cobbler, or fermenting the berries for wine.

Dried mulberries are easy to make. Place freshly collected mulberries on a food dehydrator for 6-8 hours. Dried mulberries allow you to preserve the nutrients mulberries, and much of the taste. Dried mulberries should last for three to four

months at room temperature. Mulberries can also be frozen, but frozen mulberries only last three to four months.

To make a gallon of mulberry wine, try this recipe:

## MULBERRY WINE

**What do you need:**
- ☑ 4 lbs mulberries
- ☑ 4.5 cups of sugar
- ☑ 1 tsp yeast blend
- ☑ 1 tsp acid blend
- ☑ 1 tsp pectic enzymes
- ☑ 1 campden tablet

**How to prepare it?**

1. Use all purpose or Bordeaux yeast
2. Crush the fruit in the primary fermentor and pour in all the additives and the sugar.
3. Stir well and top up to 1 gallon with hot water.
4. Let sit until cool until the Campden dissipates (about 24 hours)
5. Add the yeast and start the ferment.
6. Racking and finings as usual.

# CHAPTER 10
# POMEGRANATE

# POMEGRANATE

Pomegranates (*Punica granatum*) have been cultivated since antiquity, with ancient Biblical and Babylonian texts describing their use. Ancient tradition states that it, and not the apple, was the fruit from the Tree of Knowledge that got Adam and Eve into trouble. The pomegranate is thought to have originated in the region that includes modern-day Iran, Afghanistan, and western India. They were grown in the Mediterranean region of Europe for almost two thousand years before they were brought by Spanish conquistadors to North America in the 1500s. Throughout the colonial era in North America, in the central and Southern colonies, pomegranates were common on many farms. They are included in recreated early American gardens in Colonial Williamsburg. The first pomegranate was planted in California in the mid-1700s. Today, California is the leading state in the United States for pomegranate production, with production on many thousands of acres. Most pomegranates grown today are used for juice.

The pomegranates themselves have leathery skin and an interior full of individual seeds covered in juicy flesh. The tree is moderately vigorous, and grows best in sub-tropical to warm temperate areas. Many varieties perform best in areas with a dry climate, though the trees will produce in humid regions, such as the southeastern United States.

Virtually all pomegranate varieties require very few chill hours. They are cold hardy to about 15°F - below this temperature, the tops will die back. Temperatures below 10°F degrees will kill the roots. For this reason, all standard-sized pomegranate varieties should be planted in USDA Zones 8-10 and similar climates around the

world. Smaller, dwarf varieties that can be grown in containers and protected from harsh winter temperatures can be grown almost anywhere.

Pomegranates are considered a "superfood" due to the high antioxidant content of their juice. Pomegranate juice is increasing in popularity for this reason, and leading to more availability of the juice and fruit in supermarkets.

## Care and Cultivation

### Site Selection and Soil

Pomegranates need full sun for maximum growth. They grow bushy and tall if left untrained, so they should be planted about 10-15 feet apart. Pomegranates can also be planted and pruned into a living, fruit-producing hedge.

*The flower of the pomegranate variety 'Wonderful'*

Pomegranate Fruit

Pomegranates do well in a wide variety of soil types, as long as the soil is well-drained. Extreme pH levels in soil should be avoided. Most research shows that pomegranates do best in the neutral to slightly acidic ranges of soil pH, though they can be grown successfully in slightly alkaline (basic) soil. Pomegranates tolerate clay soil, as long as there is adequate drainage and no standing water several hours after rainfall.

**Pollination**

Pomegranates are self-pollinating, but they can also be pollinated by insects, allowing cross-pollination between varieties to occur.

### Cultivation

Pomegranates do not normally need to be thinned by hand. They will naturally drop fruit if the tree produces too much. Once the pomegranates are harvested, they will keep for up to seven months in cold storage (32-41°F.)

### Fertilization

Pomegranate trees should be fertilized for the first three years after planting with a balanced fertilizer, such as 8-8-8 or 10-10-10, applied in a circle about twelve inches from the base of the plant. Apply one ounce of fertilizer per foot of tree height in spring after growth has started. Continue to apply annual fertilizer at this rate until the tree is 8 feet tall. A soil test is recommended to prevent over-fertilization. Apply a mulch of compost or some other organic material to provide micronutrients to the tree and to retain soil moisture during dry spells.

Pomegranate trees occasionally show signs of zinc deficiency in some soils. Zinc deficiency causes the pomegranate tree leaves to yellow. If the leaves yellow without any other symptom of disease, apply a foliar zinc spray to the leaves on the entire tree. Foliar zinc sprays can be purchased from farm supply stores or online.

### Pruning

Unlike other cultivated fruit trees, pomegranates do not require annual pruning for fruit production. Pomegranate trees naturally produce suckers from the roots that can either be left to grow or pruned. If a single-trunk tree is desired, the tree should be pruned while it is still young. The developing suckers should be pruned off, leaving one or two stems that will grow into the tree trunk. Pomegranate trees grow and produce abundant fruit if left untrained. The only pruning required is the removal of dead or diseased branches; otherwise, the tree can be grown without pruning.

### Pests and Diseases

Pomegranate trees have fewer pests than other types of fruit trees. For this reason, they are an easy fruit tree to grow organically. Here are some of the more common pests and diseases that can impact pomegranates:

## Fruit Rot

The most common disease on pomegranate trees in humid areas is a fungal disease known as fruit rot. The symptoms of fruit rot first show up as dark, softened tissue on the end of the pomegranate fruit. To control the disease, monitor fruit closely as it develops. Remove any diseased fruit and destroy it promptly. If the disease continues, spray tree with a copper based fungicide at the intervals recommended on the fungicide label.

## Root-Knot Nematodes

Nematodes are microscopic organisms that feed on plant roots and deform the roots, stunting and sometimes killing the tree. Several different species impact pomegranate trees to varying degrees. There is no known chemical control available for home gardeners. If root-knot nematodes have been a problem at the planting site, remove a large amount soil from around the planting site and replace it with nematode free soil. It is best to remove soil from an area that is at least three feet across and two feet deep. Nematodes are sometimes controlled with soil solarization, but this is only effective if the soil is heated by the sun to a depth of at least six inches. Nematode populations may be reduced in soils rich in organic matter; for this reason, it recommended that pomegranate trees be mulched with compost or some other type of soil amendment at planting.

## Pomegranate Butterfly (Fruit Borer)

Pomegranate fruit borers are the larvae of a species of butterfly that lays eggs on the flowers and developing pomegranate fruit. As the fruit develops, the larvae hatches and eats its way out, destroying the fruit in the process. To control pomegranate fruit borer, spray the flowers with Malathion or Neem oil during flowering at 15 day intervals.

## Black Heart of Pomegranate

Black heart is a fungal disease that destroys the interior of the pomegranate fruit. The disease is a major problem for commercial growers. There are no symptoms of the disease on the outside of the fruit—the "black heart" is only seen once the fruit is cut open. Since the customer is usually the first once to cut open the fruit, commercial growers are concerned with the disease primarily because

it causes negative customer reactions. The interior of the fruit is inedible when the pomegranate is infected with black heart. The disease appears most often during rainy growing seasons. Good cultural practices, such as removing fallen tree material and destroying it, along with careful harvest of the fruit, can help prevent the disease. Fungicide applications have been found to not be effective. The disease may also be prevented by washing fruit after harvest and removing any discolored or damaged fruit.

### *Pomegranate Leafrollers*

Pomegranate leafrollers are an insect pest that attack pomegranate trees. The leafroller is the larvae stage of a moth that distorts and rolls the leaves of the tree. The larvae may also tunnel through the skin of the fruit, making the pomegranates unmarketable.

The damage to the leaves and fruit caused by leafrollers may make the tree susceptible to fungal diseases. Leafrollers are controlled by applications of Bacillius thuringensis every 7-10 days while the insect is present. Conventional insecticides can also be used to control leafrollers.

### Container Growing

Dwarf varieties of pomegranate, such as Nana, are perfect for container gardening. Use a well-drained potting mix in a container large enough to accommodate the tree's roots. Increase the size of the container if the roots start to get crowded.

### Propagation

Pomegranates can be propagated by seed or cuttings. Remove seeds from a ripe pomegranate and plant immediately. The seeds will sprout in warm soil quickly, but they will not be true to type, meaning they will make a pomegranate different than the parent tree.

To propagate pomegranates by cuttings, take hardwood cuttings while the tree in dormant, usually in November to January. Take 6-10 inch cuttings and plant directly in the soil outside or in a well-drained soil in a container. The cuttings should start to sprout the following spring or summer.

## Harvesting

Pomegranates are ripe about 6 months after the tree blooms. Fruit are produced only on new growth. The fruit must be allowed to ripen on the tree; when they are removed from the tree, they will not ripen further. If the fruit is left on the tree too long, the end will crack, potentially allowing rot to enter the fruit. The pomegranate is ready to harvest when the fruit can be tapped and it sounds "metallic" or has a rap to it. To avoid injuring the fruit, do not pull pomegranates off the tree. Carefully clip the pomegranates from the branch as closely as possible to the top of the fruit. This will prevent injury to the fruit. A damaged pomegranate will rot!

## Enjoying The Harvest

Some pomegranate varieties produce fruit the year of planting. Most varieties begin producing fruit when the trees are two or three years old.

Pomegranates are one of the longest keeping fruits when harvested and handled correctly. To eat a pomegranate, score the fruit all the way around with a sharp knife, beginning at the tip where the fruit was attached to the tree. Continue scoring the pomegranate until it is scored into eight sections. Cut off the calyx (protruding portion of fruit), to reveal the interior of the pomegranate. Carefully pull the pomegranate apart along the scored lines, being careful to not allow the juice to stain any important fabric. Remove the fruit tissue that is covering the clusters of seeds and gently scrape the seeds into a bowl. Pomegranate seeds, along with their red-colored surrounding membrane, can be eaten raw, added to drinks, or made into a salad.

Pomegranates can also be juiced. Once the seeds are collected, place the seeds in a plastic zipper bag and seal it. Use a rolling pin to flatten and smash the seed membranes. When the seed membranes are thoroughly smashed, cut a small hole in the corner of the plastic bag. Squeeze the bag over a glass or other container to strain the juice from the pulp and seeds. The juice is ready to drink and will keep for a few days in the refrigerator. Pomegranate juice is extremely high in anti-oxidants.

Pomegranates can be frozen whole. Place the entire fruit into the heavy freezer bags and place in the freezer. They will stay fresh up to a year and can be thawed and then used like a fresh pomegranate. Pomegranate seeds can also be frozen in freezer safe containers or freezer bags. Pomegranate seeds will keep fresh for 6-8 months.

# CHAPTER 11
# SURINAM CHERRY
## (Pitanga)

# SURINAM CHERRY
## (PITANGA)

Surinam cherry (*Eugenia uniflora*), also called pitanga or Brazilian cherry, is a tropical berry plant native to the northern parts of South America. While not a botanical cherry or a stone fruit, the plant gets its name from the textured red berry that looks like a deformed cherry as it ripens on the tree.

Surinam cherry is a tropical plant, which means it should be protected when temperatures fall below 25°F. In tropical or near tropical regions, the plant can become invasive. In these regions, care should be taken to ensure that the plant doesn't escape cultivation. The best method of control is to eat the ripe fruit before they fall to the ground to either rot or be consumed by wildlife. Any plants that come up as volunteer seedlings should be ruthlessly weeded.

The Surinam cherry is often used as a landscape plant. The flowers that cover the plant during the growing season are attractive and the plant can be pruned and kept small or allowed to grow into a medium-sized tree.

The fruit has 6-8 ridges on it and it is usually dark red - almost black - when ripe. The fruit is high in antioxidants and easy to grow.

While native to South America, where it was used by indigenous people for centuries, the Surinam cherry is now widely distributed across tropical regions of the world, including the Hawaiian Islands, India, and parts of Africa. The plant is one

of the most widely-grown hedges in Florida. In temperate regions of the world, it is best grown in containers.

## Care and Cultivation

### Site Selection and Soil

Surinam cherry can grow and produce in almost any soil type, including heavy clay and waterlogged soils. It isn't tolerant of salty soils, but otherwise withstands less-than-optimal soils with few issues. Plant Surinam cherry trees in full sun for best production, though they can tolerate partial shade.

### Pollination

Surinam cherry trees are self-fertile and will produce a crop without another tree for pollination.

Unripe Surinam cherries like these taste terrible!

One of these Surinam cherries is just about ripe.

## Cultivation

If left unpruned, the Surinam cherry can grow to heights or 25 feet or more. Maximum fruit production is from trees that are left unpruned. A full-size tree may not be practical in every situation, so the tree is often pruned in a variety of ways. Surinam cherry can take intense pruning, allowing the gardener to keep the plant as a smaller container shrub. In tropical climates, such as southern Florida in the United States, it is often grown close together and pruned as a hedge. Its attractive flowers and foliage make it an excellent landscape plant.

Surinam cherries should be fertilized at least twice during the growing season with a balanced fertilizer, such as manure-based compost or a commercial fertilizer like 12-12-12. While the plant can tolerate a certain level of drought, it should be watered on a regular basis during dry spells for maximum fruit production. Adequately watered Surinam cherry trees produce the best tasting fruit.

## Container Growing

In much of the world, with the exception of tropical and subtropical regions, Surinam cherry should be grown in containers so that the tree can be moved into a protected area during winter. To grow pitanga in containers, select a container large enough to give the roots space to grow, but not so much space that it takes years for the roots to fill the container. Use a well-drained potting mix and place the container in a sunny location throughout the growing season. Move the container into a sunny window inside during winter. Fertilize the Surinam cherry at least twice a year.

## Pests and Diseases

A few insects and diseases can negatively impact the production of Surinam cherry trees. Common garden pests, including certain caterpillars and fungi, can harm Surinam cherry trees, especially in tropical or subtropical areas. For pests such as thrips, aphids, and white flies, insecticidal soap is an easy solution. Caterpillars can be controlled using *Bt (Bacillus thuringiensis)*, an organic bacterial spray. Fungal infections should be identified and controlled with the appropriate spray if they are reducing production or threatening to kill the tree. In temperate regions, fungal diseases aren't usually an issue for Surinam cherry trees.

## Propagation

Surinam cherry is usually propagated by seed. The seeds should be taken from freshly harvested fruit and planted as soon as possible. The seeds themselves are only viable for about a month. Plant the seeds in well-drained soil; they will germinate in about 3-4 weeks.

Volunteer seedlings can be dug up and transplanted successfully in all but the hottest time of year. Seedlings will begin producing fruit in 2-5 years.

## Harvesting

The fruit develops quickly after flowering. Surinam cherries often ripen three weeks after the blooms fade. The tree will generally produce fruit in batches a couple of times each year, depending on the climate where it's grown. The average yield for a pruned mature Surinam cherry tree is about 7 pounds of fruit.

Immature Surinam cherries taste terrible and should be avoided. Fully mature Surinam cherries are so dark red that they appear almost black. They should fall off the plant at the slightest touch. These fruit are sweet and tasty and can be eaten right away or saved for making into jams, jellies, pies, and other products. The fruit does not taste like a traditional sweet cherry. Surinam cherries usually contain 1-3 seeds in the center that should be removed before eating.

## Enjoying The Harvest

Ripe Surinam cherries can be eaten fresh from the tree. They do not keep long at room temperature, but they can be refrigerated for several days. They can also be dried on a food dehydrator or directly in the sun. Place sliced Surinam cherries with the seeds removed on a medium setting in a food dehydrator for about 8 hours. Store the dried Surinam cherries in a sealed container. They should keep for a couple of months.

To make a tasty Surinam cherry jam, take 2 cups of sliced and pitted Surinam cherries and boil with a cup of water and 2 cups of sugar. Boil until thick and then can in sealed jars.

# CHAPTER 12
# WILD BLUEBERRY

# WILD BLUEBERRY

With a native distribution from Nova Scotia to Texas, the wild blueberry (*Vaccinium corymbosum* and *Vaccinium angustifolium*) inhabits many undisturbed forest edges and openings across the eastern half of North America, from eastern Texas to eastern Canada. Like their cultivated kin, they thrive in rich, acidic soils. The wild blueberry is the grandparent of the cultivated native blueberries. They are commonly found near peat bogs and in evergreen forests. They are sometimes called huckleberries. The blueberry is one of few fruits that is native to North America.

Native Americans consumed the wild blueberry in large quantities, as did European settlers. In the mid-1800's an effort was made to propagate the blueberry plants with the largest, juiciest berries. This selection gave rise to the highbush and lowbush blueberries and the domestic cultivation of these plants.

American Indians also used the leaves and berries of the native blueberry plant for medicinal purposes. Modern research has shown that an extract of the leaves may have anti-inflammatory properties.

The wild blueberry reproduces from seed in the wild, and often forms thickets. It grows along the banks of streams and rivers, in areas with an open forest canopy. This bushy plant does not tolerate shade. Wild blueberries only grow in areas with a soil pH under 6.6.

In early to late spring, the wild blueberry displays a burst of white blooms over several weeks. The berries begin ripening in early summer, and continue until mid summer.

# Wild Blueberry

Wild blueberries are an important wildlife food where they occur. The native blueberry is spread almost exclusively in the wild by wildlife droppings. Wild blueberry plants grow to between 6-12 feet in height. The plants are pollinated by bees, and are mainly self-fertile, though fruit set seems to be better with more than one plant.

Today, modern cultivars of blueberries grow on every continent but Antarctica. In the right conditions, blueberry plants are relatively care-free plants. The North American native blueberries in particular are easy to grow.

A wild blueberry relative, *Gaylussacia baccata* or wild huckleberry, is also easy to grow in the eastern half of North America and similar climates around the world, but details of its growth are not covered here.

Blueberry flowers

## Care and Cultivation

**Site Selection and Soil**

The two most important aspects of deciding where to plant wild blueberries are sunlight and soil pH. These petite berry plants need plenty of sun (8 hours + during the growing season), and acidic soil. If unsure of your soil pH, home test kits are available. It is also essential that they be watered during dry weather. Unlike some other native plants, wild blueberries are not drought tolerant, which is the reason they are so often found near creeks and streams in the wild.

Wild blueberries

**Pollination**

Wild blueberries will produce a larger crop when planted in a group of other wild blueberries. Since wild blueberries form a thicket, pollination isn't usually a problem.

## Cultivation

Wild blueberry plants thrive with minimal maintenance. In areas where well water is used for watering, make sure the water pH is not too alkaline, as this can kill wild blueberry plants over time. Occasionally, fungal diseases can affect the leaves, but this does not harm the quality or quantity of the berries. Be sure the plants are adequately watered during dry spells.

Wild blueberries tend to form thickets in the wild. In a landscape setting, this may cause concern. Wild blueberries spread by seeds and from suckers coming from the roots. They will form thickets if left alone. The usually grow to a height of 6-12

Wild blueberries in partial shade

feet in optimal conditions, and they should reach this height in 3-5 years, depending on growing conditions.

## Container Growing

Wild blueberries make great container plants. Plant wild blueberries in containers that are at least 5 gallons in size. Use a peat moss-based potting mix, or a potting mix that is known to be acidic. Water containerized wild blueberries frequently, preferably with rain water, well water, or surface water from a pond or creek.

## Pests and Diseases

In temperate regions of the world where they grow and produce, wild blueberries have no major pests or diseases.

## Propagation

Wild blueberry plants are easily removed from wild thickets in winter. Select large thickets and remove just a few plants, to ensure the survivability of the native stand. Transplanting plants during winter dormancy greatly increases the survivability of the transplants.

They are also easily propagated by seed. Wild blueberries have more seeds than their cultivated counterparts. These seeds are easily planted immediately after harvest in the summer.

For best results, place them in moist potting soil in a closed container, and place in the refrigerator for 2-3 months. This simulates winter cooling, and will force germination of the seeds.

For the more adventuresome gardener, wild blueberries can also be propagated by softwood cuttings under mist.

## Harvesting

Harvest wild blueberries when they are fully blue, usually from mid-summer in the southern half of their native range, to late summer or early fall in more northern climates. Birds and other wildlife may try to harvest berries as soon they are ripe!

## Enjoying The Harvest

Wild blueberries were sun and smoke dried by Native Americans and early American settlers. Berries were collected and those that were not eaten fresh were carefully dried in the sun. If haste was needed in the drying process, berries were smoke-dried by placing them near a fire on a clean stone.

Both of these methods would work for the home gardener today, though a food dehydrator may be a more convenient choice in modern times. Dried blueberries will last for months, and they retain all their nutritional value.

Jams and jellies made from wild blueberries are a favorite at county fairs and kitchens throughout the United States and Canada.

Like their cultivated cousins, wild blueberries are also easily preserved by freezing. Take fresh berries, without washing, and place them in freezer bags. Frozen blueberries last a year and taste great whether thawed or eaten frozen.

Blueberry muffins made with wild blueberries are a tasty treat.

Try this for excellent whole grain blueberry muffins:

# BLUEBERRY MUFFINS

**What do you need:**
- ¼ cup softened butter
- ⅓ cup sugar
- 1 egg
- 2 ⅓ cups flour
- 4 teaspoons baking powder
- ½ teaspoon salt
- 1 cup milk
- 1 teaspoon vanilla extract
- 1 ½ cups fresh or frozen wild blueberries

**How to prepare it?**

1. In a bowl, cream butter and sugar. Add egg and mix well.

2. Combine all dry ingredients; add to creamed mixture alternately with milk. Stir in vanilla. Gently fold in blueberries.

3. Fill greased or paper-lined muffin cups two-thirds full. In a small bowl, combine the sugar, flour and cinnamon; cut in the butter until crumbly. Sprinkle over muffins.

4. Bake at 375°F for 20-25 minutes. Makes 1 dozen muffins.

# ACKNOWLEDGMENTS

Writing a book like this takes research, time and experimentation – and the support of others. I'd like to thank my beautiful wife for her encouragement and constructive comments; my two precious children for their constant fun interruptive requests that I play with them; baby Eden for giving me the window of time to get the writing finished; Ethan Nelson, friend, second cousin, and fellow forest adventurer, for his editing and research assistance; my parents, who encouraged me to chase my love of gardening and writing as a child; and God, who makes things grow.

# Other Books By Trey Watson

The Lazy Gardener's Guide To Easy Edibles:
25+ Edible Plants Anyone Can Grow

The Southern Gardener's Guide to Growing Fruit Trees

Southern Bounty: How to Grow and
Enjoy Southeastern Native Fruits and Nuts

How to Grow Apples in the Southern U.S.

Loved Again

Mac The Fire Truck and The Barn Fire

Mac The Fire Truck and The Big Rig Fire

Mac The Fire Truck and The Factory Fire

Mac The Fire Truck and The Snow Cone Stand Fire

Mac The Fire Truck and The Airplane Fire

Mac The Fire Truck Saves Christmas

Mac The Fire Truck and The Field Fire

Mac The Fire Truck Omni Edition: The Compilation

# About the Author

Trey Watson grew up in East Texas where he still lives with his family. Trey has a Bachelor's degree in Horticulture and a Master of Science degree in Environmental Science, both from Stephen F. Austin State University. He is a lifelong gardener and plant fanatic.

In addition to being an author, he is also the owner of Legg Creek Farm, LLC, a nursery specializing in fruit-bearing plants for the southeastern U.S. Trey is also the author of a children's book series called The Adventures of Mac The Fire Truck.

In his spare time, Trey enjoys hanging out with his family and exploring the outdoors.

# Have a comment
## or suggestion about this book?

Email me at sales@leggcreekfarm.com

I'd love to hear your lazy gardening idea or suggestion!

*Trey Watson*

www.ingramcontent.com/pod-product-compliance
Lightning Source LLC
Chambersburg PA
CBHW042005150426
43194CB00003B/133